CARPE DIEM

SEIZE THE DAY

Sean McMahon

ILLUSTRATED

BY

MARY MURPHY

APPLETREE PRESS

First published in 1995 by
The Appletree Press Ltd
19–21 Alfred Street, Belfast BT2 8DL
Tel. +44 (0) 1232 243074 Fax +44 (0) 1232 246756
Copyright © The Appletree Press Ltd, 1995
Printed in the E.U. All rights reserved.

Carpe Diem

A catalogue record for this book is available
from The British Library.

ISBN 0-86281-516-9

9 8 7 6 5 4 3 2

Introduction

The Greeks had a word for it, people used to say, and indeed without Greek we should not have known what to call psychiatrists or physiotherapists. Now Greek is as good as dead and Latin is not feeling very well. Yet for more than two millennia these languages of classical antiquity dominated the culture and religion of the western world. Until the rise of nationalism Latin was the *lingua franca* in Europe – wherever a Latin speaker went he was understood – and within living memory acquaintance with it was the mark of the educated person.

The language of Cicero and Virgil became the language of the church. It was no accident that SS Peter and Paul set up their headquarters in the city to which all roads led. Rome had not only the most conquering army but the most pervasive civil service. So even now in its twilight we still see and use Latin in mottos, coats of arms, legal documents and impressive tags from the best authors.

This selection gives some idea of the persistence of the language of the Caesars and of its elegant succinctness. So before it makes its final exit (a word straight from Rome) it may aptly say, as did its gladiators: "Moritura, vos saluto!" (I who am about to die salute you). And we can decently respond, "Ave atque vale!" (Hail and farewell).

Carpe diem, quam minimum credula postero

Seize the day, trust least to the future

Mens sana in corpore sano

A sound mind in a sound body

Suaviter in modo, fortiter in re

Gentle in manner, resolute in deed

Veni, vidi, vici

I came, I saw, I conquered

Bellum nec timendum nec provocandum

War is neither to be feared nor provoked

Timeo Danaos et dona ferentes

Beware of Greeks bearing gifts

Veritas odium parit

Truth begets hatred

Ars longa, vita brevis

Art is long, life is short

Fama nihil est celerius

Nothing is swifter than rumour

Tempus edax rerum

Time, consumer of all things

Verbum sapienti sat est

A word to the wise

Fortes Fortuna adjuvat

Fortune favours the brave

Falsus in uno, falsus in omnibus

False in one thing, false in all

Jacta est alea

The die is cast

Roma locuta, causa finita

Rome has spoken, the cause is ended

De gustibus non est disputandum

There is no disputing tastes

Sero venientibus ossa

The bones to the late-comers

Si vis pacem, para bellum

If you want peace prepare for war

Pax vobiscum

Peace be with you

De minimis non curat lex

The law does not concern itself with trifles

Felicitas multos habet amicos

Prosperity has many friends

Semel insanivimus omnes

We have all played the fool

Corruptio optimi pessima

The corruption of the best is the worst of all

Caveat emptor

Let the buyer beware

Tacent, satis laudant

Their silence is praise enough

Vade in pace

Go in peace

Requiescat in pace

Rest in peace

$$\left(P_R + \frac{3}{V_R^2}\right)\left(V_R - \frac{1}{3}\right) = \frac{8}{3}T_R$$

Quod erat demonstrandum

That which was to be proved

Vox audita perit, littera scripta manet

The heard word is lost, the written letter abides

Ex nihilo, nihil fit

From nothing, nothing comes

Sic transit gloria mundi

Thus passes the glory of the world

Omnia vincit amor

Love conquers all

Quis separabit?

Who shall separate us?

Similia similibus curantur

A hair of the dog

Fide, sed cui vide

Trust, but take care in whom

Quis custodiet ipsos custodes?

Who will guard the guards themselves?

Ave, Caesar, morituri te salutant

Hail, Caesar, those about to die salute you

Quot homines, tot sententiae

As many men, so many minds

Divide et impera

Divide and rule

Interdum stultus bene loquitur

Sometimes a fool speaks aright

Otia dant vitia

Idleness begets vice

Natura abhorret vacuum

Nature abhors a vacuum

Habendum et tenendum

To have and to hold

Exitus acta probat

The end justifies the means

Res ipsa loquitur

The thing speaks for itself

Quem di diligunt adolescens moritur

He whom the gods love dies young

De mortuis nil nisi bonum

Say nothing but good of the dead

Nitor in adversum

Strive in opposition

Tempus fugit

Time flies

Urbi et orbi

To the city and to the world, to everyone

Hodie mihi, cras tibi

Me today, you tomorrow

Fiat justitia, ruat caelum

Let justice be done, though the heavens fall

Quem Iupiter vult perdere dementat prius

**Whom Jupiter wishes to destroy, he
first makes mad**

Quo vadis?

Where are you going?

Sic itur ad astra

Such is the way to the stars